The Swilly and The Wee Donegal

Anthony Burges

Colourpoint Books

The Swilly and The Wee Donegal

6 5 4 3 2 1

© Anthony Burges and Colourpoint Books 2006

Designed by Colourpoint Books
Printed by: W&G Baird Ltd

ISBN 1 904242 63 4
    978 1 904242 63 5

Colourpoint Books
Colourpoint House
Jubilee Business Park
21 Jubilee Road
Newtownards
County Down
Northern Ireland
BT23 4YH
Tel: 028 9182 0505
Fax: 028 9182 1900
E-mail: info@colourpoint.co.uk
Web-site: www.colourpoint.co.uk

Although English by birth Tony Burges has Irish family connections; his grandfather was from Tralee. He was very active as photographer of UK & Irish branch line railways in the period 1951–1959. He studied transportation at graduate school at Northwestern University, Chicago and photographed railways extensively in the United States. He later worked for the Canadian government as Transport Policy Advisor, Dept of Finance and Director General, Grain Transportation and Handling. He is now semi-retired and devoting time to writing railway books.

Unless otherwise credited all photographs are by the author or taken from the author's collection.

Front cover: Loco No 5 *Drumboe* makes a rousing departure from Ballyshannon (delighting visiting photographers in the process!) with a return excursion special to Donegal.   *Dr Gerald Siviour*

Rear cover: Whilst No 10 is shunting, another long established Lough Swilly tradition is maintained, namely direct transfer from rail to road transport on the platform. Further evidence of this practice lingers in the yard where a much decayed Lough Swilly bus, possibly at one time employed on the connecting service to Carndonagh, slowly disintegrates.

Introduction

The remote, largely mountainous and thinly populated county of Donegal was, not surprisingly, stony ground for the sustenance of successful railways. It was of particular interest to transport historians in that its two narrow gauge systems, operated by the Londonderry and Lough Swilly Railway (LLSR) and the County Donegal Railways Joint Committee (CDR), pursued radically different policies as far as rail transport was concerned. The former pursued a deliberate policy of conversion to road transport and has been a railway in name only since 1953, whereas the latter's rail system received stronger support from management but succumbed in January 1960. Apart from the broad gauge operations of the LLSR between Londonderry and Buncrana (opened in 1864 and converted to three foot gauge in 1885) and the Finn Valley Railway from Strabane to Stranorlar (opened in 1863 and converted to narrow gauge in 1894 when it formed the basis of the County Donegal Railway), the county was mostly narrow gauge territory. Its broad gauge lines were limited to short sections of the Great Northern Railway (Ireland) (GNR). The GNR left Strabane for Derry and crossed McKinney's Bridge, a metal structure across the Foyle, about two miles out. There were then three stations – Porthall, St Johnston and Carrigans – before the line crossed the border again for the last 2½ miles to the Craigavon Bridge in Derry. The other section of broad gauge in the county was the portion of the GNR's Bundoran branch west of the border at Belleek. Today, the county is bereft of railways with the exception of preservation efforts at Fintown on the former Glenties branch of the Donegal Railway and at Donegal Town.

There was a sense of desperate urgency on my only visit to the Lough Swilly. Closure was just over four and a half months away and there was some sense of uncertainty as to whether the goods trains would run according to timetable. Life in this period of rapidly accelerating railway closures in Britain and Ireland was fraught with these now or never panic situations, but one travelled hopefully. So on arriving by Great Northern in Derry there was no alternative but to take the Londonderry and Lough Swilly Railway bus from the city to Buncrana. It seemed a little odd at the time for a bus to carry the name of a railway company, but as the route generally paralleled the railway there were some tantalising glimpses to be had from the upper deck of the Leyland vehicle. The discovery that shunting was in progress at Buncrana was a great relief and provided a leisurely opportunity to inspect this northern terminus of the truncated system. From 1901, the line had been extended northwards from Buncrana up the Inishowen peninsula to Carndonagh. Another longer extension carried Lough Swilly trains westward in 1903 from Letterkenny through very rugged and lonely country to Gweedore and to Burtonport on the Atlantic coast.

It should be remembered that in the 1950s there were only three places, apart from Derry, on the Lough Swilly system with a population exceeding 1000. These were Letterkenny, Buncrana and Moville and the latter was only served by the company's bus and road haulage services. The Lough Swilly rail network had been steadily withering on the vine with the Carndonagh line being replaced by road services in 1935, followed by the sections linking Gweedore to Burtonport in 1940, and Letterkenny to Gweedore in 1947.

The occasional passenger was still tolerated on the remaining freight trains of which there were two in each direction from Derry to Buncrana and Derry to Letterkenny on weekdays. Dilapidated passenger rolling stock was retained until the end for a few weekend excursion specials to Buncrana. The Buncrana–Derry goods called at all stations except Beach Halt and Lisfannon Golf Links halt, both of which had an air of dereliction about them. Nonetheless, there was a significant amount of freight business until closure, confirmed by the number of vans awaiting Customs clearance at the border station of Bridge End. There was a pleasant interlude in a scenic setting on arrival at Tooban Junction to cross a Letterkenny bound freight which passed at a surprising speed. The terminus at Londonderry Graving Dock and the atmosphere at Pennyburn shed and workshops did little to dispel the all pervasive gloom that had settled on the line in its final days. Soon the powerful locomotives of the Lough Swilly would become nothing more than memories. It is a trifle disturbing to recall that more than fifty years have elapsed since the company completed its long planned conversion to that of a purely bus and truck operator, a task which in itself continues to be an exercise in careful cost control to ensure survival.

A journey across the city of Londonderry brought one to another narrow gauge terminus.

Victoria Road station on the east bank of the river Foyle, and adjacent to the bi-level road and rail bridge connecting the two sections of the city, was something of a contrast to the LLSR establishment at Graving Dock. The station with its wide platform was quite commodious and well maintained. The steam-hauled passenger train which followed a purely Northern Ireland route southwards to Strabane was notable for its fresh paintwork, although the absence of passengers suggested that travellers preferred the more frequent service offered by the GNR(I) from Derry to Strabane. It was to be no great surprise when this section of the CDR was closed in January 1955.

On reaching Strabane the scene changed radically. It was obvious that the CDR was a serious railway with a mission to provide a high level of service to the extensive territory it served. There seemed to be more activity on the Donegal rather than the GNR(I) side of the sprawling station, with railcars dominating the passenger services westwards to Letterkenny and southwest to Stranorlar, Donegal and Killybegs. *Phoenix*,

that unique steam/diesel rebuild of Clogher Valley ancestry, was fully employed on shunting duties and Donegal steam power was much in evidence on freight services. Northern Ireland Customs were busy checking arriving passengers on the Donegal platform. It had something of the air of one of the more progressive French secondary railways; the Reseau Breton immediately leapt to mind.

The railcar from Strabane to Letterkenny was well patronised and the Irish Customs examination at Lifford was completed quickly. Letterkenny, and the intermediate stations of Raphoe and Convoy, were handling a healthy amount of freight traffic and there was evidence that the CDR appreciated the benefits of containerisation as a means of alleviating the delays attributable to change of gauge. I particularly relish the memory of the solid exhaust beat of loco No 6 *Columbkille* as it struggled out of Letterkenny, on wet and greasy rail, with a goods bound for Strabane.

On the main line to the west from Strabane there was a pause at Castlefinn where trestle tables on the platform heralded the inevitable Customs check before the run to Stranorlar, the nerve centre of the system and location of the workshops for the maintenance of both rail and road equipment, as well the seat of administration. Here one could reflect on the similarities and contrasts with the Lough Swilly. The lengthy branch line to Fintown and Glenties, which joined the main line at Stranorlar, had been closed one year earlier. The territory it served was as big a traffic desert as the Burtonport extension of the Lough Swilly. But beyond the wild and scenic Barnesmore Gap there were significant passenger and freight generators at Donegal, Ballyshannon and Killybegs. Yet, like the LLSR, the CDR made extensive use of road-based feeder services. However, the economics of the freight business on the CDR were generally more attractive on account of the population of the area served and its close working relationship with the GNR(I). The Donegal was a strong proponent of seasonal excursion business particularly to the coast at Rossnowlagh and Ballyshannon and these steam-hauled special trains were very popular.

The journey from Donegal to Killybegs provided a good opportunity to observe just how successful the County Donegal was in maximising the small amount of business that existed. Railcars stopped at certain level crossings, thus bringing the service as close to the customers door as was feasible. Supplementary bus services were based on the GNR(I) bus garage adjacent to Donegal station and it was always a pleasure to inspect such a smart and well maintained, if often elderly, fleet of vehicles. The harbourside railhead at Killybegs overlooked what is now one of Ireland's leading commercial fishing ports and bus services were provided to western extremities of the county at Glencolumbkille, Malinmore and Portnoo.

The County Donegal was unlike any other railway in Ireland. It was an object lesson in the successful operation of a narrow gauge line in difficult terrain where traffic was scarce. Its extensive reliance on railcars reflected European practice and its staff heeded the message contained in its working timetable:

> *REMEMBER! It is well for each Member of this railway to bear in mind that goodwill based upon years of conscientious effort may be entirely destroyed by a moment's carelessness or indifference toward a customer.*

Since the disappearance of its railways, County Donegal's population has grown and its tourist and manufacturing sectors have expanded. However, even such a committed lobby group as Platform 11, with its mission to strengthen the role of rail transport in the Irish Republic, does not seriously envisage the restoration of any rail connections to Co Donegal as being feasible in the foreseeable future.

Selected Bibliography

Patterson, Edward M, *The Lough Swilly Railway*, David & Charles/Macdonald, 1964

Patterson, Edward M, *The County Donegal Railways*, David & Charles/Phoenix House, 1962

Acknowledgements:

My thanks must go to Dr GR Siviour of Attleborough, Norfolk for kindly making available his photographs, and to Michael Bowie of Lux Photographic Services of Carleton Place, Ontario, Canada for breathing new life into my fifty year old negatives. I am also extremely grateful to Norman Johnston and Paul Savage at Colourpoint Books for turning my text and photographs into this splendid book and to Joe Curran for providing useful additional information.

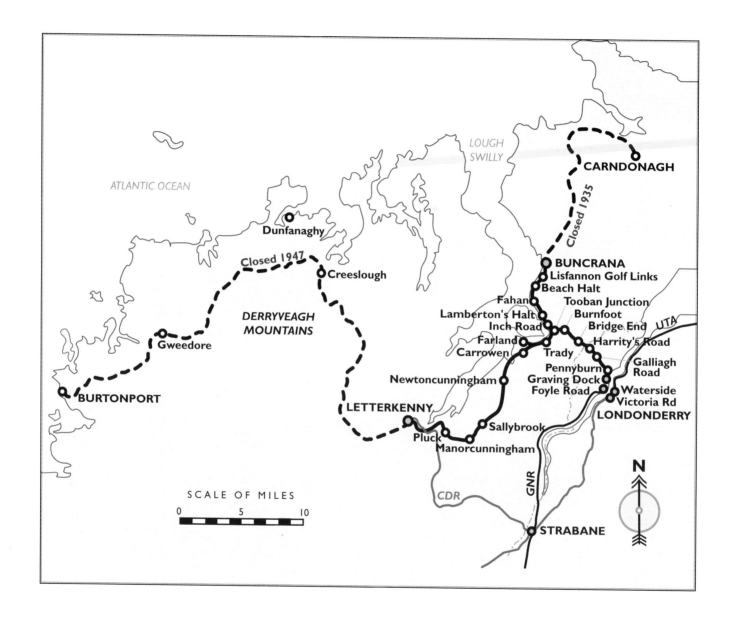

ATLANTIC OCEAN

LOUGH SWILLY

CARNDONAGH

Closed 1935

Dunfanaghy

Closed 1947

Creeslough

BUNCRANA
Lisfannon Golf Links
Beach Halt
Fahan
Tooban Junction
Lamberton's Halt
Burnfoot
Inch Road
Bridge End
UTA
Farland
Harrity's Road
Carrowen
Trady
Galliagh Road
Pennyburn
Graving Dock
Foyle Road
Waterside
Victoria Rd
LONDONDERRY

DERRYVEAGH MOUNTAINS

Gweedore

BURTONPORT

Newtoncunningham

LETTERKENNY

Pluck
Sallybrook
Manorcunningham

SCALE OF MILES

0   5   10

CDR

GNR

STRABANE

N

We start with a general view of Buncrana station on Tuesday 31 March 1953, looking in the direction of the Carndonagh extension. The wide platforms and footbridge at Buncrana station were once thronged by day trippers from Derry and, during the Second World War, crowds of rowdy British servicemen, attired in civvies, and in search of smokes, booze and unrationed goods of all descriptions. An erstwhile railway customer, which outlived the railway was the Railway Bar. Its essential supplies journeyed from the Guinness brewery in Dublin by the Great Northern Railway (Ireland) to Derry for transfer to the Lough Swilly. Doubtless the taste was improved by a period in bond whilst in transit!

The Lough Swilly made an assertive architectural statement with its station building at Buncrana. It would appear that a local farmer has parked his Ferguson tractor whilst partaking of refreshment in the Railway Bar! In 2006 the building is still in public use – as a bar and restaurant.

Whilst No 10 is shunting, another long established Lough Swilly tradition is maintained, namely direct transfer from rail to road transport on the platform. Further evidence of this practice lingers in the yard where a much decayed Lough Swilly bus, possibly at one time employed on the connecting service to Carndonagh, slowly disintegrates.

Interesting survivors on the Derry-bound goods on Tuesday 31 March 1953 were wagons lettered L&BER (for the Letterkenny and Burtonport Extension Railway, the last portion of which had been closed six years earlier).

The hills of Inishowen and the shore of Lough Swilly as seen from the 11.00am Buncrana–Derry goods near Lisfannon Golf Links on that morning in March 1953. Only freight trains featured in the last working timetable issued, dated 3 March 1952. Three trains departed from Londonderry each weekday, two for Letterkenny and one for Buncrana.

Fahan, formerly a port of call for steamers on Lough Swilly, possessed the largest station building between Derry and Buncrana. The existence of a pub within the station was of greater significance locally than the rapidly fading railway. The Lough Swilly had, at one time, operated a ferry service from here to Rathmullan. The company had a long tradition of being multi-modal with interests in rail, road and water transport.

The small wayside station of Inch Road was, like its counterparts on the Lough Swilly, presided over by a crossing keeper – a cost which may have done little to enhance the viability of the remaining remnants of the Lough Swilly network in the 1950s.

No 10, with the 31 March 1953 morning Buncrana–Derry goods, waits at Tooban Junction for the Letterkenny train, pictured opposite, to pass. The signalman was kept remarkably busy, even though closure was nigh.

Tooban Junction, where the lines to Buncrana and Letterkenny diverged, occupied a picturesque, if windswept, setting and was accessible by footpath only. Loco No 15, built by Hudswell Clarke in 1899 for the long abandoned Buncrana–Carndonagh extension, raises the echoes as it approaches with a Derry–Letterkenny goods. Beyond are the hills that form the backbone of the Inishowen Peninsula.

Burnfoot station was situated one mile before Bridge End and there was evidence of some limited freight traffic here until the end.

No 10 is seen at Bridge End in March 1953, with the morning goods from Buncrana. It is likely that the vans in the loop here have been detached from earlier westbound trains due to insufficient time being available for the completion of Customs clearance. The watering facilities here were used to top up locomotives when shunting was completed.

Bridge End, four miles from Londonderry (Graving Dock), was the first station in the Irish Republic and Lough Swilly trains were subject to, sometimes lengthy, Customs examination. The shunting associated with this process was usually a good opportunity for the photographer.

4-6-2T No 10, built by Kerr Stuart in 1904, is busy shunting at Pennyburn after arriving with the freight from Buncrana. The third class bogie coach served as a brake van and conveyed the occasional railway enthusiast. It was one of twelve such vehicles built by Pickerings of Wishaw, Scotland for the Burtonport extension in 1903/4.

Once the departure point for weekend revellers, summer tourists and returning countryfolk, by March 1953 Londonderry (Graving Dock) station was showing signs of its diminished status, prior to the abandonment of all Lough Swilly rail operations in August that year. In the early 1950s, Londonderry was still served by four passenger carrying railways (two broad gauge – GNR(I) and UTA – and two narrow gauge – CDRJC and LLSR). Each railway maintained its own terminus in widely scattered parts of the city. Now only one of these stations (that of Northern Ireland Railways, the successor to the UTA) remains, and for more than fifty years the Londonderry and Lough Swilly has been a purely bus and road freight operation.

Despite not having operated a train for over fifty years the Londonderry and Lough Swilly Railway Company is still in existence and still providing passenger and freight services in the north of Co Donegal, perhaps vindication that the company's deliberate policy of conversion to road transport was indeed the right one. My journey from Londonderry to Buncrana back in 1953 was on a Lough Swilly Leyland bus and in 2006 that Leyland tradition continues. Here, Lough Swilly No 423, a Leyland Leopard with Alexander 'Y type' bodywork, is seen at Lackagh Bridge, near Creeslough, in May 2005, during an enthusiasts' tour of abandoned Lough Swilly bus routes. This vehicle was new to Western Scottish, Kilmarnock in May 1980 and arrived with the Swilly in December 1999.

Paul Savage

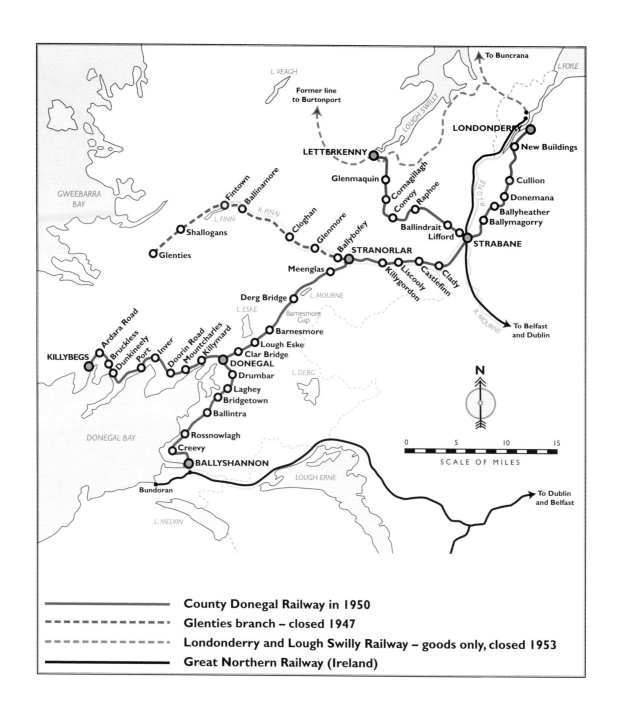

County Donegal Railway in 1950
Glenties branch – closed 1947
Londonderry and Lough Swilly Railway – goods only, closed 1953
Great Northern Railway (Ireland)

Victoria Road station, situated on the eastern bank of the River Foyle, was the newer of the narrow gauge termini in Londonderry. The adjacent bi-level Craigavon Bridge provided a mixed gauge link to the GNR(I), UTA & LLSR systems. Normally services of the County Donegal Railways Joint Committee to Strabane were steam hauled. Class 5 2-6-4T No 6 *Columbkille* awaits departure for Strabane with a mixed train on 31 March 1953.

23

This is Cullion station, seen from a Londonderry–Strabane mixed train on Tuesday 31 March 1953. Cullion is in County Tyrone, 6¼ miles from Derry and 8¼ miles from Strabane. The station opened in August 1900 and closed on 1 January 1955, when the CDRJC route between Derry and Strabane closed.

Strabane was an important border station and junction, where the broad gauge GNR(I) connected with the County Donegal Railway. The extensive station site was divided between the companies. In this view from the north end, on Saturday 31 August 1957, most activity is confined to the Donegal platforms where railcar No 15 has arrived from Stranorlar and diesel loco No 11 *Phoenix* is performing its regular shunting duties.

Having commenced its career as an unsuccessful steam locomotive on the Clogher Valley Railway, No 11 *Phoenix* was converted to diesel traction (powered by a Gardner 6L2 engine) in 1932, following purchase by the CDRJC, the conversion work being undertaken by the Great Northern. *Phoenix* spent most of its time at Strabane where it handled freight and mail interchange traffic with the Great Northern, positioned vans for Customs examination and shunted passenger rolling stock. As a unique type of steam to diesel conversion it more than earned its keep over the years. *Phoenix* is currently on display at the Ulster Folk and Transport Museum, Cultra, Holywood, Co Down.

Seen at Strabane in the summer of 1957, locomotive No 11 *Erne* was one of four class 4 Baltic 4-6-4Ts built by Nasmyth, Wilson in 1904. These powerful locomotives handled much of the heavier freight traffic on the Strabane–Killybegs and Strabane–Letterkenny lines. This engine was re-numbered from 14 in 1937 and was scrapped at Letterkenny c1967, although it had been purchased by a Dr Cox for use in the United States. No 11 was the last Baltic tank in the British Isles and had worked the track lifting train to Letterkenny.

The Great Northern route between Londonderry (Foyle Road) and Strabane ran through County Donegal, crossing the border twice. After 1 October 1958, staff at the three intermediate stations – Carrigans, St Johnston and Porthall – were in the unusual situation of wearing CIÉ uniforms but having their stations served only by Ulster Transport Authority trains! Here, Great Northern PP class 4-4-0 No 71 detaches cattle wagons at Strabane on 31 August 1957, while a porter waits before wheeling what may be a barrowload of homing pigeons to the Donegal platforms. Beyond, passengers await the arrival of a service from Stranorlar.

The Finn River bridge, seen here on Saturday 31 August 1957, also spanned the international boundary between Strabane and Lifford and was the largest structure on the Letterkenny line. No 6 *Columbkille* (No 18 *Killybegs* before the 1937 renaming and re-numbering) and a Letterkenny–Strabane freight await Customs release at Lifford station.

With a full-fronted cab that enclosed its diesel engine, railcar No 20 had a semi-streamlined appearance that was the last word in modernity when delivered to the 'Wee Donegal' in 1951. En route from Strabane to Letterkenny on Saturday 31 August 1957, it is undergoing Irish Republic Customs examination at Lifford. Built by Walkers of Wigan, railcars Nos 19 and 20 were the Donegal's newest pieces of passenger equipment and were destined to survive closure for a continued, if uncertain, existence on the Isle of Man. The bridge across the River Finn and the railway right of way through the station were subsequently converted to a temporary road for use by replacement bus services.

A deserted Ballindrait station is seen from a Letterkenny–Strabane goods train. The line between the two towns opened on 1 January 1909 and closed completely on 1 January 1960. Ballindrait was 2¾ miles from Strabane.

Class 5 2-6-4T No 6 *Columbkille*, built by Nasmyth, Wilson in 1907, pauses at Raphoe on 31 August 1957 to attach additional wagons. Visitors were carried in the brake composite coach that also did duty as a brake van and so they had ample opportunity to study Donegal shunting practices.

Raphoe was 6½ miles from Strabane and 12¾ from Letterkenny. The removal of the passing loop was an obvious sign of earlier rationalisation at this station. Like all the other stations on this line it closed on 1 January 1960.

A well loaded freight from Letterkenny to Strabane, with nine miles left to run, passes through Convoy station on Saturday 31 August 1957.

In 1957 the former wool town of Convoy still generated freight business for the Donegal. Water for locomotives was available at Convoy, Raphoe and Letterkenny, the water tower at Convoy being just to the right of the engine in this view.

Restricted space on the platform roads at the Donegal's station at Letterkenny sometimes resulted in a railcar being consigned to a siding between runs, as had happened to railcar No 20 on 31 August 1957. In 2006 the County Donegal station building at Letterkenny is still in use as the Bus Éireann office and station, the area viewed here being the bus parking area and a shopping centre car park. The roof of the former Lough Swilly station is visible beyond railcar No 20.

Under the shadow of Oatfield's confectionery factory at Letterkenny on the same day, No 6 *Columbkille* is about to leave with a goods for Strabane. The County Donegal Railways were handling small inter-modal containers of biscuits from Dublin, as can be seen on the loading dock.

No 6 *Columbkille* is working hard as it leaves Letterkenny with a Strabane goods.

Westbound passengers were subject to open air Customs examination at Castlefinn, after leaving Strabane. Railcar No 14, a product of Walkers and the Great Northern in 1935, is towing two vans forming a Strabane–Killybegs service on Saturday 31 August 1957. In wet weather it is doubtful if the morale of the passengers would have improved after Customs clearance.

Stranorlar was the headquarters of the County Donegal Railways Joint Committee system. Railcar No 15, another product of Walkers of Wigan and the GNR(I) workshops, pauses en route from Killybegs to Strabane on 31 August 1957. The line was opened in stages between 1863 and 1893 and closed throughout in January 1960.

Twenty-one coaches were all that remained in 1957, out of the original fleet of 59 vehicles. Many of the withdrawn coaches were converted to wagons whilst scrapping accounted for the balance. By the end of 1957 a further two vehicles had been withdrawn. The remaining 19 coaches, which were retained for excursion service, or as brake vans on freight trains, survived until closure in 1960 when they were sold to a private buyer or preserved. Part of the strategic reserve of passenger vehicles awaits the call at Stranorlar in the late summer of 1957. All three coaches seen here were built by Oldbury, the two furthest from the camera being composites Nos 14 and 16 dating from 1893. The closest is No 47, a third class compartment coach built in 1907, subsequently modified to include guards accommodation.

Compartment coach No 58 was formerly a corridor vehicle built in 1928 by the LMS (NCC) for the Ballymena–Larne boat trains. It arrived on the County Donegal after its transfer from the abandoned Ballymoney–Ballycastle line in 1951. Here it is stored on the former Glenties branch platform at Stranorlar. The line between Stranorlar and Glenties opened on 3 June 1895 and closed to passengers and regular goods services on 15 December 1947. It closed completely on 10 March 1952.

The County Donegal fleet was further enriched by the arrival of a 35 hp petrol railcar from the Dublin & Blessington Steam Tramway in 1934. It was numbered 3 and was subsequently converted to a 40-seat trailer in 1944. It is seen here at Stranorlar in August 1957. It is now preserved at the Ulster Folk & Transport Museum, Cultra, Co Down.

It is clearly a 'soft' day in the Blue Stack Mountains as railcar No 12 approaches Stranorlar on a Killybegs–Strabane service in August 1957. The former Glenties line diverged to the right. Most of this area is now occupied by the offices, garage and bus parking area belonging to the state-owned bus operator, Bus Éireann. When I last visited, some of the telegraph poles to the left of the picture were still standing and part of the Glenties platform could be discerned.

Dr Gerald Siviour

Donegal was a busy rail and bus passenger interchange. On 31 August 1957 railcar No 14 is receiving passengers for the Killybegs line while No 19 has just arrived from Ballyshannon. Part of the station building, on the right, is now in use as a railway museum. Bus Éireann also has offices and bus parking facilities at this location.

Class 5 2-6-4T No 5 *Drumboe*, built by Nasmyth, Wilson in 1907 as No 17 *Glenties,* takes water at Donegal. Re-numbering and renaming took place in 1937. At the closure of the system No 5 was bought by a Dr Cox for use in the USA but was never shipped. It is currently on display at the Donegal Railway Heritage Centre at Donegal station (see www.cdrrl.com/).

Railcar No 14 pauses at Inver, 8¼ miles from Donegal, to unload some parcels whilst en route to Killybegs on Saturday 31 August 1957. No 14 was built by the GNR and Walker Bros and entered service in February 1935. It seated 41 passengers and was powered by a Gardner 6L2 diesel engine. The Donegal to Killybegs section opened to traffic on 18 August 1893 and closed, with the rest of the system, on 1 January 1960.

During the stop at Inver I was fortunate to be able to photograph trailer No 6 about to be removed from railway property, having been sold out of service. No 6 had been new in 1930 as a Great Northern/O'Doherty petrol railcar and was rebuilt as a four-wheeled trailer in 1945. One wonders how many chicken houses in County Donegal have railway ancestry!

This is the interior of the weatherworn trainshed at Killybegs. Railcar No 14 has just arrived from Strabane and, after unloading its passengers, etc, will run forward to the turntable.

This is the view of the harbour end of Killybegs station. Its exposed harbourside location, in one of Ireland's most important Atlantic coast fishing ports, was reason enough for the County Donegal Railway to offer passengers additional protection from the wind and rain. The CDRJC had a goods platform and shed at Killybegs (behind the photographer) and there was also a line down on to the pier for delivering oil to the fishing fleet. The rails remain in the pier to this day.

After arrival at Killybegs diesel railcar No 14 was turned for the return run to Strabane. It was commonplace for these railcars to tow one or two vans and to perform shunting duties at intermediate stations. The turntable was constructed on the chassis of 2-6-4T No 19 *Letterkenny*, although prior to 1950 the chassis of a Class 2 4-6-0T had been in use. The location of the turntable was just beyond the trainshed.

Railcar No 14 awaits departure time at Killybegs on 31 August 1957. The average running time to Strabane was 3 hours 5 minutes. Extended scheduled stops at Donegal, Stranorlar and Castlefinn accounted for 20 minutes of this total. A further 23 stops were theoretically possible on demand. On this basis and considering the rugged gradient profile of the line an average speed of about 17 miles per hour was quite creditable and the Donegal was a good timekeeper.

This is the view east from Killybegs station, back towards Donegal, with the CDJRC's small, one road, loco shed in the centre distance. The shed was demolished in 1957 when No 6 *Columbkille* ran away. Note the rodding for the signal running alongside the wall on the right. Killybegs signal box was behind the photographer, on the seaward side of the line.

The way ahead – the view from half-cab railcar No 14 at Bruckless while en route from Killybegs to Strabane. By rail, Bruckless was 4½ miles from Killybegs and 46 miles from Strabane. On the closure of the system in 1960. No 14 was stabled at Stranorlar and did not survive. It was scrapped in 1961.

Back at Donegal railcar No 19 is about to be turned on the turntable. Note, too, the rudimentary refuelling facilities. Powered by a Gardner 6LW diesel engine, and costing £8176, No 19 took up service in January 1950. Seating was provided for 41 passengers. No 19, along with slightly younger sister No 20, are now resident on the Isle of Man, stored out of use.

Class 5 2-6-4T No 5 *Drumboe* heads a crowded excursion train to Rossnowlagh and Ballyshannon at Donegal during August 1957. Adjacent to the station is the Great Northern Railway (Ireland) bus garage. This area is still used for bus parking by Bus Éireann, successor to the GNR(I).

Dr Gerald Siviour

As well as a rail presence in the county, the GNR(I) operated numerous bus services, providing connections between principal towns and villages. Services operated in the 1950s included Ballyshannon–Donegal–Portnoo, Carrick-on-Shannon–Bundoran, Killybegs–Glencolumbkille–Malinmore, Ballybofey–Letterkenny, Stranorlar–Glenties–Portnoo, Glenties–Dungloe and Derry–Raphoe–Sligo, on which run timetabled journeys took approximately 4½ hours. In the summer of 1950, the single fare for the last mentioned journey was 12s 0d. No 269, seen here resting at Donegal on Sunday 1 September 1957, was a 1954 AEC Regal IV 9822E with GNR bodywork on Park Royal frames.

Dissatisfaction with the products of the major bus manufacturers led the Great Northern to produce its own vehicles at Dundalk from 1937. Ninety-six were constructed up to 1952. They had Kirkstall axles, Leyland gearboxes and the reliable Gardner 5LW engine. Waiting outside the garage at Donegal are two of the 'Gardners', as they were universally known. On the left is No 328 while the one on the right is No 243. No 328 was one of a batch, Nos 318–330, built in 1941/2 with timber-framed bodies, which later had to be rebuilt due to the poor quality of the timber used.

Inside the garage at Donegal three buses are seen undergoing maintenance. The only one readily identifiable is No 387, which was new in 1950. The bodywork is again by the GNR on Park Royal frames. Nos 361–384 had bodies by Harkness of Belfast on Metal Sections frames. On takeover by CIÉ, No 387 became G387 and survived until 1978 by virtue of having been converted to an ambulance for use at the Knock Shrine in Co Mayo. Most other Gardners had been withdrawn by 1964.

Railcar No 19 is about to leave Donegal for the Ballyshannon branch in this shot taken in the late summer of 1957. Trains for Ballyshannon, to the south and Strabane, to the north, both left Donegal in the same direction, the routes splitting just to the northeast of the station.

This is the end of the line at Ballyshannon where the stationmaster's house was a notable feature. The limited siding accommodation here could be strained when steam hauled excursions were operating. Ballyshannon had two stations, the CDR one being located on the north side of the town. The other was the GNR(I)'s, on the branch to the seaside resort of Bundoran. The church in the background is St Anne's Church of Ireland.

Perhaps the occasional dose of carbon must have made the pastures at Ballyshannon station all the more irresistible to the cattle! Railcars Nos 19 and 20, new in 1950 and 1951 respectively, represented the ultimate in modernity on the Donegal. No 19, built by Walker Bros and GNR(I), is in the midst of the armstrong turntable ritual before heading back to Donegal.

Trailers were used to provide additional passenger capacity on railcar services when required. Trailer No 2 is seen here near the large wooden goods shed at Ballyshannon on Saturday 31 August 1957, awaiting its next call to duty. This trailer seated 30 and had been rebuilt in 1944 from the ex-Castlderg and Victoria Bridge Tramway petrol railcar which had been lying out of use at Glenties for the previous three years. The railcar had been purchased in 1933 for the sum of £25.

Loco No 5 *Drumboe* makes a rousing departure from Ballyshannon (delighting visiting photographers in the process!) with a return excursion special to Donegal.

Dr Gerald Siviour